Alla
Napier
MacNab

John M. Bas
A. Roy Petr

Fitzhenry & Whiteside Limited

Contents

© 1974 Fitzhenry & Whiteside Limited
150 Lesmill Road,
Don Mills, Ontario, M3B 2T5

Printed and bound in Canada

ISBN 0-88902-201-1

York in Chapter 1
Flames

The crash of splintering timbers nearby brought young
Allan MacNab to his senses, and, without thinking, he
backed away from the window. He had been fascinated
by the scene he was watching. Already several buildings
near the wharf were on fire. The cause was obvious:
small white puffs of smoke appeared from time to time
from the line of ships off Scarborough Bluffs.

The drums had been beating a steady tattoo for almost half an hour, and men had been running in re-
sponse to its alarm. Most were local militia, equipped
only with musket and powder horn, or occasionally a
bandoleer loaded with ball shot. The regular troops had
already marched off toward the shore to meet the landing
which was certain to follow the bombardment.

The War of 1812-14 was now in its second year, and so
far things had gone quite well for Canada. Brock and his
Indian allies had been successful in beating back American invasions. They had even managed to capture Fort
Michilimackinac and Detroit. They had not been so successful at sea, however. Britain was blockading
Napoleon in Europe, and had no ships to spare. Because
of the lack of ships, the Great Lakes were largely in
American hands. This had contributed to the defeat at
Moraviantown, where Tecumseh died. Now, York was
under siege.

Fort York (later Toronto)

Allan would dearly have loved to join the men rush-
ing to push back the American invaders. But his father
had wisely locked the lad of fifteen in his room, with a
stern warning to stay there. Nevertheless, the imprisonment annoyed young Allan, who figured he was big
enough to serve his king and country.

The drums had stopped now, but the boom of distant
cannon still echoed off the walls. Allan tried the door
once more, but it was still locked. He cursed softly and
cautiously inched his way toward the window.

Why do ships go line astern *for such an attack?*

Artillery pieces during the War of 1812

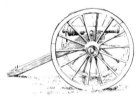

Light field gun

6-pounder field gun

Bronze field cannon

The thick glass, with its bubbles and distortions, never gave too clear a view. Now the panes were cracked by the cannonade, making it even more difficult for Allan to see. It was obvious, however, that whaleboats bearing landing parties were nearing the shore. Plumes of white water marked the return fire from the defenders, but the wave of invaders swept on.

The crackle of musket fire marked the arrival of the American forces on the beach, and continued for what seemed an age. Strain as he would, Allan could see little now, but the continuing fire told him resistance was still very active. The pall of smoke had spread, which worried him even more. However, there was nothing he could do but wait.

After what seemed another endless period, Allan could see men re-embarking along the shore and rowing swiftly back to their ships. Just as quickly, the ships hoisted sail, turned about, and headed down the harbour without further attack.

Now a key was turned in the lock, and Allan rushed to meet his father. He was sweating, untidy, smeared with black powder stains, but unharmed. "What happened? Have they left? Did we win?" Allan directed this torrent of questions to his father whose only answer was, "Come and see for yourself."

Allan hurried down the steep stairs and went into the street. Men were straggling back now. Some were helping the wounded to a nearby inn, which had become an emergency hospital. Other men were running with ladders and buckets, to try to put out the spreading fire. Women, with young children clinging to their skirts, were anxiously seeking out their menfolk.

Damage was visible everywhere. Huge fallen timbers blocked practically every street. There were gaping holes in many of the principal buildings. The new government buildings were already burnt out, and were clearly beyond the efforts of struggling bucket brigades.

There had not yet been time to see about the bodies of soldiers from both sides, which lay around in queer heaps. The sight of the blood and the bitter smell of smoke in his throat eventually drove Allan back to the greater safety of the outskirts of York, the village-capital. His father returned to do what he could to help put out the fires and bury the dead. Allan would return to fight another day, but this black April 27, 1813, burned itself forever on his brain.

Allan, hungry for excitement, turned down shore to the main fortress. The place looked like a slaughter-house. A huge crater, black and smoking, marked the spot where the fort's ammunition store had stood. "What happened here?" Allan shouted at the sentry guarding the spot.

The man, pale and shaken, replied, "Ah, lad, this is no place for ye! The place reeks with death and destruction."

"I can see that!" retorted Allan, somewhat annoyed. "But how did it happen?"

"No one quite knows. But the whole thing blew up, killing the American General, Zebulon Pike, and over 250 of his men," said the guard. "It's the main reason they retreated so quickly," he added cautiously, as he spotted the officer of the guard approaching. "Now run along with ye, lad," he urged, "before I get myself in trouble with this officer!"

Reluctantly, Allan moved off, full of wonder, but eager to strike back. For the moment the enemy had won.

Tecumseh at the Battle of the Thames, Moraviantown, 1813

Attack on York

1. What was the range of naval guns in 1813?
2. Why has the range of artillery been increased so enormously in 150 years?
3. What American cities were burned in revenge for the burning of York?

A Middy Chapter 2
Strikes Back

Almost a year later and half a head taller, Midshipman Allan MacNab strode the deck of Commodore Sir James Yeo's flagship, the 112-gun, 2,300-ton *St. Lawrence*, with his telescope tucked firmly under one arm. They were headed straight for Sackett's Harbour, to destroy the American naval supplies stored there.

A stiff breeze snapped the spanker. The ship lurched slightly, forcing young Allan to catch his balance on his newly acquired sea-legs. He wasn't sure the sea was his element, but he welcomed any opportunity to strike back at the enemy. "Keep making those soundings as we approach shore," he bellowed.

"Aye, aye, sir," the seaman replied.

Britain, though a great sea power, had been constantly unsuccessful on the Great Lakes. This was largely due to under-gunned ships and too few trained sailors. This voyage was no different. There was scarcely a man aboard the *St. Lawrence* experienced enough to steer a ship of this size, let alone engage the enemy. However, no naval battle was expected. The crew's job was to land a force of marines and militia, and to provide covering fire.

Young MacNab put his glass to his eye and surveyed the approaching shoreline. "No sign of the enemy fleet, sir," he reported to his superior officer. "The harbour looks almost empty, except for a few barques and merchant schooners. There appears to be a large work party busy on the quay, however," he continued. "I wonder what's in those large wooden containers? The men are so busy, they don't appear to have noticed us yet."

Another half-mile closer to shore, and the whole picture changed rapidly. A loud boom was followed by a whistling shot, which passed high over their main sky sail.

"Hard aport and bring her to bear on 130 degrees," the captain shouted.

The shot landed well astern with a mighty splash, but Allan felt more secure because he was on a weaving target.

"Bearing 130, sir," the helmsman reported. "Steady as she goes," replied the captain. At the same time the work party ashore scurried in every direction to take up defensive positions.

"To your stations," Allan commanded. The men for whom he was responsible obeyed. Gun covers dropped open, and ugly black snouts stuck out of each. "Load your guns, but hold your fire until the order is given," Allan instructed. No other word was spoken. They would close a little more, to make sure every shot found its target. The soldiers were not exposed, but took cover in the well of the vessel until the seamen were ready to launch their assault boats.

24-pound cannon

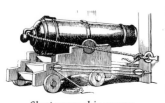

Short-range ship cannon

Allan, himself, was outwardly calm, although his heart beat faster, and he could feel a vein throbbing in his neck. Once more he gazed at the shoreline. He stood with his legs apart and his head erect. He was proud to be there.

At this moment, one of the ships in the harbour chose to run for it. This was a mistake. "Fire!" came the order. The resulting salvo rocked the *St. Lawrence*, but it was accurate. The fleeing enemy vessel was hit.

"Reload, and fire at will!" Allan shouted. The order was scarcely needed. The second round brought the foremast crashing in a tangled mess on her deck. "That should slow her down," shouted Allan excitedly. "Well done, my buckoes," he added, as the American ship burst into flames, and a series of sharp explosions tore her in two. "She's done for!" cried Allan, as she keeled over and sank like a stone. "She must have been loaded with ammunition for the Yankee troops," Allan shouted joyfully to his fellow officer, who nodded in agreement.

The shore batteries were becoming more accurate now; several men were wounded by the ball shot which was scattered over the deck. "Launch the assault boats," the Midshipman shouted. It was essential to get the landing parties afloat quickly, and pull the *St. Lawrence* back out of range. "Steady on that forward tackle" rang out. But, here again, lack of experience took its toll: several whalers were smashed in the launching.

The passage seemed to take an endless time to those

on deck. But to Midshipman MacNab, who was in command of one of the landing craft, everything seemed to happen in an instant. "Pull together, lads," he urged, "and hold your fire for the moment."

Musket fire was now never ceasing. Several of Allan's party were struck, in spite of their attempts to keep below the side of the boat. "Take over the rudder and see to that man," he snapped, as yet another was hurt. "Head for the shelter of that jetty, where we can take cover."

His instructions were to wait, once his party was ashore, even though he longed to join in the battle. Suddenly, there was an enemy soldier lunging at him. "That is for York!" bellowed Allan, as he slashed the man's arm with his cutlass. The man collapsed in a pool of blood. Leaping over him, Allan fired his pistol into some powder spilling out of a broken cask. Immediately the jetty burst into flames.

In a few moments, under a cloud of drifting smoke, his party withdrew. Their mission was finished. "Revenge is sweet," Allan murmured to the nearest man.

"Aye, that it is, sir," he replied.

British and American ships
clash on Lake Ontario, 1813

Battle of Lake Erie, 1813

Chapter 3 **Aftermath**

The war ended almost as quickly as it had begun, although it dragged on in Europe. Neither side could claim to be the winner. But the independence of the Canadas was established once and for all. Allan was glad to have taken part in it. However, even though he was discharged on half-pay as a veteran ensign, this did not mean that he was sure of a good job.

As happens after most wars, the country suffered a mild depression. Allan, who was still only eighteen, had no real trade, although he worked for a time as a carpenter, a part-time actor, and a manager of real estate. He drifted from job to job. All the while he was piling up debts, which at last caught up with him.

"I'm sorry, Mr. MacNab, but you'll have to come with me," said the burly constable.

"But I'll pay those debts," said Allan. "All I need is a little time."

"You heard what the magistrate said," replied the jailer. "You are to be sent to York Prison until your just debts are met."

"But how am I to pay, if I'm imprisoned here?" protested Allan.

"I can't say, sir," murmured the constable. "Perhaps your friends can help."

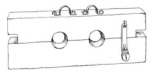

The stocks, a form of punishment in use at the time Allan was in prison. What other forms of punishment were used for prisoners?

The heavy iron door clanged behind him. Allan, his eyes adjusting to the gloom, looked at his new surroundings. It was a big room, with rough stone stretching up fifteen feet or more to a small window. Dim rays of light filtered through its bars. A dozen other prisoners were scattered about the room. They were of different ages, some old and some young, but none younger than himself. Most were lying down on piles of straw, or had pulled a harsh blanket around them. One or two sat on a rough bench attached to a heavy wooden table. There was little other furniture in the room, except a wooden bucket in the corner, which served as a latrine. The smell of this, and the stale dampness, almost sickened Allan.

"How long have you been here?" Allan asked one middle-aged man.

"Three years almost to the day," he replied, coughing badly.

"Have you been ill?" Allan asked, with concern.

"Almost everyone in here is sooner or later," said the man. "It's the damp and cold, you know."

"Do you expect to get out soon?" was Allan's next question.

"If I can raise the money I owe," the prisoner answered.

"Have you friends or relatives who can help?" continued Allan.

"Not a living soul," confessed the man between sobs that shook his whole body.

Allan felt sad, but he determined to make the best of things. Another lad named John, who was a few years older, made friends with him. They sat on a heap of straw, and shared a loaf of bread and a little cheese he had been able to buy with the help of the jailer.

"How long have you been here, John?" asked Allan.

"Only about six months," John said, "but I lose track of time occasionally. Is this September?"

"Yes," said Allan, "it's the third."

"Then it's almost seven," mumbled John, his voice trailing off absent-mindedly.

"Were you in the war?" inquired Allan.

"Yes, I was a sergeant in the Queen's Own," replied John. "But they soon forget the veterans, once the war's over."

"Do you hope to be free soon?" asked Allan

"I've written to my uncle, who lives in Kingston. But the mail takes a month or more, so I don't know how soon," answered John wearily.

Evening had come, and only a flickering lamp cast its shadows from the corridor. The jailer paid regular visits to the barred door, to watch the prisoners. The evening meal of thick potato soup and heavy grey bread had been filling, but was not satisfying. Already Allan felt quite hungry.

At last, the prisoners huddled together for warmth on a dirty straw mattress. A few threadbare blankets scarcely served to cover them. The cold autumn air crept through every crack in the walls, to the marrow of Allan's bones. He slept off and on. Several times, he woke to hear the scurry of rats, looking for the crumbs the poor wretches had missed. Once he woke, when a cockroach crawled out of the straw bed across his face.

Morning came, and with it some thin porridge and a black brew called coffee. Allan's arms and legs were stiff and aching, but exercise in the courtyard, which was surrounded by a high wooden stockade, soon got the kinks out of them.

"What's the routine for the day?" Allan asked John.

"Half an hour out here, and then back into the cell," he replied. "It's not much, but it's better than rainy days when we exercise in the corridor."

"Do we have work to do?" Allan inquired.

"Only to try to tidy our quarters, and there's precious little we can do about that," John complained.

The days passed slowly, and Allan had lots of time to think. He decided that, to be a success, two things were necessary: he must remain within the Family Compact, and he must, somehow, get a bit of money.

The Family Compact was an alliance of wealthy families who supported the Tory government and the Church of England. Allan knew several of its members, and he was certain he could count on their friendship. Although the MacNabs were poor, their family had owned land in Scotland. Allan, therefore, belonged by birth to the Family Compact. He realized, too, that to get money, he would have to establish himself in a profession and invest in land. Both of these aims would be easier if he had the help of influential friends. Allan's father had his own money troubles, and could do nothing for his son.

Finally, after two weeks' imprisonment, several of Allan's Family Compact friends were able to raise the money to pay his debts, and he was released from the notorious York jail.

"Good-bye, John, I won't forget you," shouted Allan, as the big door closed behind him. "If your uncle's money doesn't arrive soon, I'll be back to set you free."

Who was chiefly responsible for prison reform?

Not only was Allan as good as his word, but he determined he'd help the others, once he had made his fortune and gained a powerful position. Fortune was to smile on him soon. This cruel experience was not wasted on the future lord of Dundurn.

1. When did imprisonment for debt end?
2. What other punishments were severe by today's standards?

York Jail

Chapter 4 **The Lawyer**

The Hamilton Courthouse, in use from the early 1830s until 1879

Lady MacNab, Sir Allan's second wife

Allan had had his experience of the wrong side of the law. Now he was destined to gain a profession on the right side. In 1816, he was articled as a copying clerk in the law office of Attorney-General D'Arcy Boulton, a family friend. He did well, so that when he met a girl called Elizabeth Brooke, he was able to get married. They had two children: Robert Allan, born in January, 1823, and Anne Jane, born in 1825. Unfortunately, the young mother died shortly after the birth of her daughter. This was a frequent tragedy in those days.

But, on the whole, those were happy times. Allan was seeking a new start. He had qualified as a lawyer in 1826, and needed to build up a practice. He decided to move to a place known as Hamilton, in a land-locked harbour at the head of the lake. So, with only four dollars in his pocket and two children to care for, he set out for the community he would help to build.

"Where's the new lawyer's place?" a voice inquired.

"Just around the corner on James Street," another answered.

These words floated through the window of his new office. Allan peered out of the window, through the young willow trees lining the street. *Here comes my first client*, he thought.

His practice grew. While most cases concerned property and wills, he did occasionally deal with criminal matters, involving theft, fraud, and even murder.

Law at that time was not the learned profession it is today. Allan often found his meagre training had not been enough. Nor were law books easy to get. Often, they had to be imported from England, which was expensive. Previous verdicts in British law also formed the basis of many decisions in struggling Canadian courts. Justice was rough, but it served the people well.

Allan enjoyed his practice which flourished. But the money he was making came largely from his position as a land officer, and from wise investments in real estate. Before long, he was one of the district's largest land-owners. In 1831, he married again. His bride was beautiful Mary Stuart, and they had two daughters, Sophia and Mary.

"Where are you heading today, Allan?" asked his neighbour, a merchant, noticing his hurry.

"I hope to see one of my dreams come true," replied Allan rather impatiently.

"Another land deal?" persisted his friend.

"I cannot say at the moment," replied Allan, "but you'll all know soon."

And so they did. For on that day, Allan MacNab bought the property once owned by Richard Beasley, reportedly the first settler on the bay. It was to become the site of the magnificent Dundurn Castle.

Mary MacNab, Sir Allan's youngest daughter

Sophia MacNab

Sophia MacNab kept a diary from the age of thirteen. This drawing is one of many in it. What is the picture about?

Chapter 5 **Building Dundurn**

Allan MacNab stood on the edge of the high bank of the shoreline of Burlington Bay, and looked across the land he had bought from John Cartwright for £2,500. The thousand acres had originally belonged to Richard Beasley, who had cleared 150 acres, and built a house there, where he had lived for 35 years.

The thoughts running through Allan's head were certainly not those of a Scot careful with his money. His dream was to build a smaller copy of his grandfather's family house, Dundurn Castle, which overlooked beautiful Loch Earne in Scotland.

"I want the building to be constructed right over the foundation of Beasley's house," Allan explained.

"Where can we get stone for such a house?" asked Robert Wetherell, the architect who had designed the proposed castle.

"There is excellent limestone on Dundas Mountain," replied Allan.

"Good!" exclaimed Wetherell enthusiastically. "Then we can begin as soon as the stonemasons arrive."

"I've engaged a man called John Allen from Staffordshire, England, to oversee the job," remarked Allan.

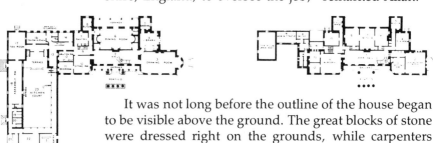

Robert Wetherell's ground floor and second floor plans for Dundurn Castle

It was not long before the outline of the house began to be visible above the ground. The great blocks of stone were dressed right on the grounds, while carpenters faced heavy wooden beams with broad axes and adzes. Allan was there every moment he could spare from his office, to supervise the building.

"I hope to include many of the Greek and Roman styles I learned from my teacher," Wetherell told him.

This was done to prevent the spread of the disease in a family, or so that the neighbours would not know which house was affected. No one would go near anyone suspected of having been in contact with cholera.

The doctors, few as they were, were helpless. They knew nothing about germs, which caused cholera. They thought it was due to "unwholesome air." The common treatment was to bleed the patient and give him doses of calomel and opium. This, of course, was completely useless.

Cholera raged throughout Asia. It was, therefore, called Asiatic cholera. British troops in India brought it to Afghanistan, and from there it spread to Russia. The sickness went through Europe and reached England in October, 1831. Ships carrying Irish immigrants brought it to Canada. It was no coincidence that cholera broke out in 1832 and 1847—the two heaviest immigration years.

In 1832, 66,334 immigrants came to Canada. They were packed in the ships like sardines in a can. They had little or no sanitary arrangements, fresh air, or enough food and water. Many died aboard ship before reaching Canada. Those poor unfortunates who survived the eight-week journey were then dumped ashore at various ports, without lodgings or shelter for the healthy, let alone the sick.

The citizens were furiously angry. On one occasion they actually used pitchforks and clubs to force the new arrivals to stay in the dock area. In the end, immigration sheds were built, but these hardly provided protection from the weather, and became pesthouses themselves. There was no medical aid for the sick, and many of the families preferred to sleep in the open fields.

Why are immigrants kept on Ellis Island in New York Harbour?

"Cholera has broken out in the jail," announced his clerk, on Allan's arrival at the office one morning.

"Have they released the prisoners?" Allan demanded, remembering his own sad experience in a similar jail.

"They say they have no power to do so," replied the clerk.

"Power be damned!" spluttered Allan, as he stormed out of the office and headed for the jail.

On reaching the jail, Allan went straight to the jailer, who was uncertain what to do. "Release them immediately," Allan commanded. "I'll go bail, and my friends and I will be accountable for their good behaviour." The jailer immediately obeyed, glad to have someone make the decision for him.

But the decision came too late for the jailer. Both he and his wife, and one woman debtor, died of cholera. In all, 600 perished in Hamilton alone, or about one in twenty of the population. Farmers refused to bring their produce to market, adding to the food shortage. Many merchants closed their shop doors for the summer. Mercifully, the beginning of the cold weather brought the epidemic to an end.

But the summer of disaster had not ended. One night, Allan was awakened by a cry of "Fire!" in the street. There was the clatter of running feet, and the noise of the fire-reels hauled by the snorting horses. "Where is it?" demanded Allan.

"In the heart of town, they say," replied his servant. Allan pulled his boots on. Wrapping himself in his coat, he joined the surging crowd going toward the glow in the midnight sky.

And there it was —his new tavern wrapped in flames. "How did it start?" asked Allan.

"No one seems to know," a voice replied.

"Is anyone inside?" demanded Allan, with real concern.

"They think not," said someone else in the crowd, "but it's spread to the post office and several stores."

"Perhaps this will burn out the cholera," remarked still another stranger, not realizing what the loss meant to Allan.

It was obvious to Allan that the fire would have to burn itself out. All they could do was to prevent it spreading further. In the morning, only the gutted and smouldering ruins remained. Apart from Allan's tavern, six buildings were destroyed, including the offices of the Desjardin Canal Company and the *Western Mercury*; the store of Ferguson and Company; the post office; the house and shop of Mr. Scobie, and Mr. Miller's tavern and outbuildings.

"No sense crying over spilt milk," Allan told his business partners. "It has been a bad year, but a good one to have behind us. From now on, I'm going to concentrate on politics and completing the castle." It would be three years yet, however, before he could hold the house-warming.

1. Why are plagues of this kind very unlikely to occur **The Plague**
   in Canada these days?
2. What other plagues have you heard of?

Chapter 7 **Member for Wentworth**

While his castle was being built, and during the cholera outbreak, Allan MacNab sat as the member for Wentworth in the Legislative Assembly of Upper Canada. His political career began as the result of a public scandal, and the arrest of several prominent Tories, including Colonel Titus Simons, Dr. James Hamilton, and Allan himself. In spite of lack of evidence, they were jailed for contempt when they refused to give any information to a Select Committee of the House investigating the charges.

"I cannot but feel myself accused, tried, and convicted unheard," Allan said heatedly.

"Did you or did you not help to tar and feather George Rolph of Dundas, a member of the Reform Party?" demanded the chairman of the Select Committee.

"Sir, I must respectfully claim the protection of the rights by birth of every Canadian inhabitant," replied Allan.

"Were you with Colonel Simons and Dr. Hamilton on the evening of the attack on Mr. Rolph?" asked the chairman once more.

"I refuse to answer, on the grounds that I do not have to testify against myself," retorted MacNab.

"It is obvious to me that you have no intention of assisting this inquiry," concluded the chairman.

Once more Allan found himself in York Prison. This time, cholera made it even more horrible. He knew what to expect. But he believed a principle was at stake, and he refused to involve his friends and fellow party members. "After all," he said privately, "these upstart fellows preaching reform and the destruction of the Family Compact must be taught a lesson!"

The days that followed crept by slowly. Prison conditions had been improved, but they were still far from comfortable. Warmth came from a box stove of cast iron in the centre of the cave-like room.

"The heat from that stove takes the darkness out of the air," said MacNab, "but it doesn't throw the heat very far. And the smoke it gives off catches one in the throat."

"That's true, but I'd hate to be without it tonight," stated the prisoner next to him.

"We all huddle close to it, and to one another, on these cold nights," added another, "and even then you roast on one side and freeze on the other."

One morning, as the sun began to creep up the wall, the jailer appeared at the barred door. He ordered Allan and three others to step forward.

"You're free to go," the jailer announced.

"Have we been pardoned or acquitted?" demanded Allan.

"I'm afraid not," replied the jailer, "but your friends have raised the bail necessary to set you free."

Outside the jail, Allan and his friends were met by a small band of rejoicing supporters. "Welcome back!" shouted one of them. "Elect MacNab to the Legislature," screamed another at the top of his voice. Several others took up the cry. Lifting Allan onto their shoulders, they marched down the street shouting their slogans as they went.

And so, in the election of 1830, Allan MacNab became the Tory Member for Wentworth. He was to hold the seat without a break for the next twenty-seven years.

"I promise to uphold the crown, the constitution, and established religion," thundered Allan MacNab to the crowd on election night. The upturned faces were rosy with the light reflected from flaming torches. At this statement a roar went up, and Allan came down from the platform and climbed into a waiting carriage. A sea of outstretched hands reached out to shake his. Allan's popularity was obvious, and it grew with every year.

The band struck up a march; the banner bearing MacNab's name was lifted up high; and the parade moved from Gore Park to a garden party in the grounds of Dundurn, which was still in the building stage. Allan's new career had begun very well.

Chapter 8 A Castle for the Chief

The year 1835 arrived with merriment and celebration. The memory of the horrors of cholera had faded, and times were relatively flourishing. Light shone out over the crisp snow, which creaked under the wheels of carriages as they drew up to the entrance of the newly completed Dundurn. A housewarming was underway and the cream of "society" was at the party.

"Come in out of the cold," called Allan from the entrance hall. "It's a bitter night, but there's warmth from the fire and the punch bowl."

The front hall was magnificent with its massive circular staircase leading upstairs, its rich wallpaper, fine gilded mirrors, and the thick carpet. Wraps were taken by the waiting servants, and the Laird of Dundurn led his guests into the main dining room.

Here was an even more beautiful scene. A heavy and exquisite chandelier hung from the high ceiling. Light from the crystal and silverware danced on the ceiling. In one corner several musicians were playing a lilting waltz. Ladies, in long and lacy gowns, and gentlemen, in velvet and linen, sipped a spiced rum punch from silver cups.

When all the guests had arrived, they were invited to the main ballroom to receive greetings from the Chief of Castle Dundurn.

"A hearty welcome to all my friends and neighbours," began Allan. "I trust you will have an enjoyable evening in our new home and that this will be only the first of many happy times for you under this roof.

"And, now, let the dancing begin," invited Allan, and the orchestra began to play a schottische.

"May I have the honour of this dance?" MacNab begged one of the ladies. She accepted; they began to dance, and others quickly joined in.

As the evening wore on, some of the gentlemen drifted off to the games room for billiards, or for indoor bowling on very fine alleys near the rear of the home.

Others gathered in the library to chat before a roaring fire of huge logs, while a servant brought a fresh tray of deep red wine in long-stemmed glasses.

"You must join me this summer for some cockfighting," Allan said to one of the gentlemen.

"But isn't that illegal?" he asked in surprise.

"Perhaps so," laughed Allan, "but they'll have a hard time finding my cockpit, as it is hidden away in the grounds."

It was well past midnight when the guests left. It had been a highly successful party, not likely to be forgotten. But it was only one of many which would brighten the halls of Dundurn over the coming years.

Hall
This is called a floating staircase. How was it constructed?

Drawing Room
Why were mirrors difficult to manufacture in the mid-nineteenth century?

Restored Dundurn Castle

Bedroom
What sort of lamps can you see?
What fuel was used? What is
unusual about the bed?

Dining Room
Would the MacNab family
breakfast in the dining room?

Chapter 9 **Speaker of the House**

Upper Canada had been seething throughout the 1830s. William Lyon Mackenzie, Marshall Spring Bidwell, and Dr. John Rolph, members of the Reform Party, were attacking the government unmercifully. The matter came to a head in 1836, when the Assembly refused to vote the Supply Bill, which was needed to pay government salaries. The Lieutenant-Governor reacted by vetoing Bills to improve roads and education. The result was a minor economic depression and a financial crisis.

William Lyon Mackenzie

The appointment of Sir Francis Bond Head as Lieutenant-Governor in January, 1836, had been a dreadful mistake. Although considered a "tried reformer," he soon made enemies of even moderate Reformers. They resigned from his Executive Council (a small body of personal advisers). He quickly labelled all Reformers "traitors and Republicans," and hailed the Tories as loyal and devoted to the British Crown.

The Assembly was in an uproar. Members shouted across the floor at one another, in spite of the attempts of the Speaker to keep order. "Stop behaving like a dictator," screamed Mackenzie at the Governor, shaking his red wig in anger.

"Give us true responsible government, and make the Council answerable to the Assembly," demanded William Warren Baldwin more moderately.

"The moment we do that, we will have broken our connection with the Mother Country," argued Allan MacNab from the Tory benches. "Perish the thought," added John Beverley Robinson, another devoted Tory.

"Force that upon us and we'll have the vengeance of 150,000 loyal and true men," threatened Solicitor-General Hagerman.

After just two days of such hatred and venom, it was obvious that no constructive legislation could result. Bond Head acted in the only way he knew. He dismissed the Assembly in May, 1836, and called a general election.

Bad as this action was in itself, Head made it worse. He actively campaigned for the Tories and declared all Reformers disloyal, when he was supposed to remain neutral.

Allan MacNab was back as a candidate in Hamilton. "Elect the Reform candidate," declared Allan, "and you'll all be part of the United States within the year." He then went on to attack the Opposition, accusing it of godlessness and disloyalty to all that Canadians stood for. "They'd destroy the established church, and with it would go the defences that protect property and British liberties, for which our forefathers fought and died," warned Allan.

The Tories did not stop at such exaggerated statements. They used bribes. Farm labourers said they received four dollars to vote Tory, as well as a ticket claiming they owned property. The ticket qualified them to vote. Others said that squads of Orangemen, loyal to the Family Compact, beat them up when their politics were known, or forced them with threats to stay away from the voting stations.

As a result, the Reform Party was defeated. Speaker Bidwell was defeated in Lennox and Addington, Peter Perry took a beating, and even William Lyon Mackenzie lost by one hundred votes in the Reformist riding of York. The majority of seven the Reform Party had held in the Assembly was reduced to a minority of twenty-five.

Bond Head now had the Assembly he wanted. This "bread-and-butter" Assembly met in November, 1836. Allan MacNab was appointed Speaker. Assured of their majority, the Members voted the Supplies Bill and a number of Bills for public improvements. But they were nervous, for financial conditions improved very little. Mackenzie and the more radical Reformers despaired of legal means to remedy their complaints. They were openly preaching rebellion, and were secretly drilling for it.

Allan Napier MacNab
Speaker of
the House of Assembly

Chapter 10 **Saviour of York**

It was December, 1837. Armed men were moving about in the night. They were a mixed crowd, dressed in homespun and armed with muskets, pitchforks, and fishing poles with carving knives tied on top. It was hardly an army to carry out a successful rebellion.

Inside Montgomery's Tavern on Yonge Street, north of the city, the leaders continued to argue about what they should do.

Which side would you have taken in the 1837 Rebellion?

"I tell you we must strike now," argued Mackenzie. "The city is defenceless. All we have to do is seize the Lieutenant-Governor and take the City Hall. A large quantity of ammunition and arms are stored there and in Fort Henry, at Kingston. We can take it easily."

Some of the more moderate looked nervous at Mackenzie's bold proposal. "That tastes of treason, and I'm not your man if this is your plan," declared Dr. Morrison, a Reform Member of the Assembly and former Mayor of Toronto. The notary, Mr. Elliott, Doel the brewer, and others agreed, and the meeting broke up without a decision. Such a golden opportunity for success would not occur again.

Rebels drilling in North York, 1837

Rebellion already had broken out in Lower Canada. Bond Head, thinking Mackenzie was bluffing, had sent all available troops to help in that province. This had left Toronto without defences. Captain, now Colonel, James FitzGibbon, of Beaver Dams fame, was left with a corporal's guard at the fort and the Governor's residence. He tried his best to persuade Bond Head to call out the local militia. But the Governor refused, fearing such a move would merely arouse trouble.

Rumours of unrest continued to reach FitzGibbon's ears, and he urged the Governor to take action.

"For God's sake, Your Excellency," pleaded FitzGibbon, "call out the militia and citizens loyal to the Crown."

The Governor just awakened from his sleep, and still somewhat cross, steadily refused.

"But, sir," FitzGibbon urged, "a traveller just arrived reports hundreds of armed men ready for attack on the city's outskirts. We are defenceless against such a force in our present state."

Bond Head gave a curt, "No." Returning to his bedroom, he gave strict orders that he was not to be disturbed. FitzGibbon was in a rage!

Others were not so easily put off, however. Allan MacNab, as he boarded the ship for Hamilton, promised FitzGibbon that he would return in the morning with a loyal force.

True to his word, he mounted his fast horse, "Sam Patch" (named after a famous acrobat), and rounded up sixty or more "Men of Gore," members of the Gore District Militia. On December 6, 1837, they sailed from Hamilton on the *Experiment*, arriving in Toronto before nightfall.

Now Mackenzie, with all the supporters he could expect, received reluctant consent from his associates to march on Toronto. However, he, Captain Anthony Anderson, and three other mounted men decided to try to find out what was happening in the city. As they approached Toronto they met Alderman Powell and one of his friends and captured them. Powell had a pistol hidden on him. Turning suddenly, he fired directly at Captain Anderson, hit him in the neck, and killed him outright. He then fled back to Toronto to give the alarm. This time, Bond Head was convinced, and FitzGibbon was allowed to go into action.

The sword given to Allan MacNab by the "Men of Gore"

All the bells in Toronto were ringing now. Men were scurrying about like ants when their hill is disturbed. Muskets were being handed out to members of the Family Compact, and riders were sent to summon MacNab and other officers on half-pay, and loyal militiamen.

What followed was like a farce. Mackenzie's advancing riflemen were met by a round of gunfire from twenty-seven men under Sheriff William Jarvis' command. Mackenzie's experienced troops in front returned the fire, and then dropped to the ground to give the next rank a clear aim. The inexperienced men behind thought the front rank had been completely wiped out. So they turned and fled. Jarvis' men did the same. Neither Mackenzie nor Jarvis could get their men together again, and the affair became a flight in opposite directions.

Mackenzie's troops stopped only when they reached Montgomery's Tavern once more. Meanwhile, Colonel MacNab had arrived with his Men of Gore, and he and FitzGibbon were given joint command. Mackenzie placed his remaining troops under old Colonel Van Egmond, who had come from Goderich. Van Egmond, a veteran of the Napoleonic Wars, scattered the men in a nearby wood to await the attack.

"Here they come!" shouted a sentry. Mackenzie and Van Egmond galloped to higher ground, to see more clearly. "There's company after company of them," mumbled Mackenzie.

"They've got cannon, too," observed Van Egmond.

"Split into two columns on either side of the road," ordered FitzGibbon. This was a good move, and showed his experience. "Fire!" commanded MacNab, and several of the militiamen's shots found their marks.

The rebels began a slow retreat, some dropping their weapons as they went. Then the cannon roared, and grapeshot burst over the trees, spraying the rebels below. A cannon ball burst through the window of the tavern and out the other wall. Unarmed rebels swarmed out like hornets and fled into the surrounding fields.

Mackenzie and the other leaders fled on horseback northward, to escape capture. The battle was lost in less than half an hour. Poor Van Egmond was taken prisoner. The rebellion was broken. Sir Francis Bond Head declared that MacNab was "The Saviour of York."

Fugitive Chapter 11

"Have you seen Mackenzie or any of his rebels?" the officer on horseback demanded, while several of his men prodded the haystack with their bayonets.

"Neither hide nor hair of him," replied the settler, fully aware that Mackenzie was listening to everything from behind his pigsty.

"Remember he's wanted for treason, and there's a thousand pounds reward for his capture," warned the officer. "Remember also that anyone offering him shelter or help is guilty, too, and will be hanged." He turned and rode off with his men.

When the coast was clear Mackenzie and his companion came out. Having thanked the farmer sincerely, they set off on foot toward Niagara.

A number of people they met on the way recognized him immediately, but all were friendly. Some offered him food and shelter, and one provided him with a ride to the next friendly homestead.

Hardly had they started down the road, when they spotted an armed patrol. "Give me those reins," yelled Mackenzie, shoving the servant aside.

"Across that far bridge," shouted his companion, "and head for the wood beyond." The wagon lurched across the bridge, losing a wheel as it struck a large boulder. "Dive for it," Mackenzie urged, shoving his companion headlong into a hedge. A hail of shot fell around them. "That was close," said Mackenzie breathing heavily.

"Too close for comfort," agreed his friend, as he sat on the ground and rubbed his bruised and scraped legs.

They left the woods just before daybreak, and asked a farm hand to direct them to a nearby village. "That will throw them off the track," smiled Mackenzie, as they pushed on toward the Sixteen Mile Creek.

When they reached the stream, it was swollen with melting December snows and freezing cold.

"There's nothing to do but to try to cross it," said Mackenzie.

"I'm afraid so," agreed his companion. He stripped off his clothes to prepare for the horrible swim.

The water proved even colder than they had expected. Chunks of ice hit them as they crossed. They stifled their cries of pain, for fear of disclosing their whereabouts. Numb and tired out, they stumbled ashore on the other side.

Mackenzie was able to find another friendly farmhouse, but his companion was suffering from shock and exhaustion, and had to be left behind. Mackenzie went on alone, but the new-fallen snow betrayed every step he took.

"I'd like to help you, friend," said one farmer from whom he sought shelter. "But the countryside is crawling with MacNab's men. They've already searched my place twice today, and they're making terrible threats about anyone caught helping you."

"I understand," sympathized Mackenzie, "but thank you, anyway, for the warning."

And so it went, until, while eating dinner at a farmhouse, Mackenzie met Samuel Chandler, a wagonmaker of St. Johns in the Short Hills.

"I insist on conducting you to the border myself," said Chandler.

"Thank you for the offer," said Mackenzie, "but you risk the noose."

"It's worth the risk," replied Chandler. "After all, you've risked everything for us."

On reaching the Niagara River bank, they found all the skiffs had been seized. Chandler went to look for a Captain McAfee, who had a boat and agreed to ferry them to Navy Island. The boat was launched. As they stepped in, they heard the sound of horses' hooves.

"There's Colonel Kerby, the Customs Officer, and a troop of green-coated dragoons," whispered McAfee.

"Pull away quickly before they spot us," urged Mackenzie, "or the game is up."

"Hello there, Colonel Kerby," shouted Mrs. McAfee from her doorway, thus distracting his attention. Meanwhile, the fugitives pulled rapidly into the swift current, out of range of the guns.

"Another close call," breathed Mackenzie, relieved to reach the safety of the island's shore.

The Burning of the Caroline Chapter 12

Allan MacNab was thoroughly annoyed. Mackenzie had escaped, and had set up a tiny republic on Navy Island in the middle of the Niagara River. From there he hoped to recruit American support, re-invade Canada, and eventually succeed in his rebellion.

"I'm leaving immediately to take command of the troops and besiege the island," Allan told the Governor.

"You are commissioned to do so, Colonel MacNab, and I wish your campaign every success," replied Sir Francis. "One word of caution, however: be careful to do nothing to annoy the American government."

By noon, Allan had left by sled to take command. It was to prove the highlight of his career, and would result in his being knighted by Queen Victoria for his services to the Crown.

Once on the frontier, MacNab had no intention of being careful. It was obvious that Mackenzie was getting stronger each day. Recruits were flocking to him, and the Americans were on his side.

"Their defences don't appear very adequte" commented Allan, looking through his telescope.

"They don't have to be, sir," replied his Adjutant, "as the current is very swift, and anyone attempting to cross would be a sitting duck."

"How do they receive their supplies?" inquired Allan.

"By ship from the American shore," answered the officer.

"Is that a supply vessel I can see moored on the opposite shore?" continued Allan.

"Yes. She is the *Caroline*," said the Adjutant.

"Could she be cut loose?" asked MacNab.

"At night, it would not be difficult," remarked his companion.

"Then we'll do it!" determined Allan.

Commander Drew, who led the expedition against the Caroline.

"But the opposite shore is American territory," warned the officer.

"We'll do it, anyway. Desperate situations need desperate action. Call me when the next watch is set, and alert Commander Drew of the Royal Navy and his boarding party," ordered Allan MacNab.

"Yes, Colonel," answered the Adjutant.

About midnight, seven small boats made the crossing with muffled oars.

"They suspect nothing," the Colonel whispered to Commander Drew. "She's all lit up like a Christmas tree, and not a guard in sight."

"My party will crawl up the anchor chain," suggested the Commander, "and yours can board her from the wharf."

"I agree," said Allan, "but be quick." Allan and his men crept stealthily up the gangplank and onto the poop deck. At this moment, one of the crew of the Caroline was unfortunate enough to come out from the hatch. He cried out in alarm. A pistol barked behind Allan, and the man lunged forward in a pool of blood.

"Round up the others quickly," the Colonel commanded.

"Cut the lines," ordered Commander Drew, as one of his men tossed a lighted bundle of sticks into supplies piled on the deck. A great burst of flame arose, casting its flickering light on the waters.

The small steamer of forty tons was drifting into the river. On shore, men could be seen running with lanterns toward the wharf, shouting to each other as they ran.

"Put the prisoners into one boat, and cast off," ordered Commander Drew.

"Boarding party cast off," rang out.

As they rowed rapidly away, the flames leapt higher, casting an eerie glow over the water. The ship was moving quickly now, as the current caught her, and she descended the rapids toward Niagara Falls.

"There she goes!" shouted the men joyfully, as the flames suddenly disappeared. The Caroline had gone over the brink.

Allan was joyful, too. Though he had risked war with the United States, calmer heads were able to prevent it, and Mackenzie's hopes of conquering Canada faded forever. He would go into exile for the next twelve years, and the United States, under President Van Buren, would take action against the Americans who had encouraged him.

Honours were heaped on the man who was now Sir Allan Napier MacNab. Sir Francis Bond Head wrote, "I congratulate you on your success, which is no more than I expected from you." The Duke of Wellington, in the British House of Lords, declared that, "owing to the loyalty, zeal, and active intelligence of Sir Allan MacNab the Canadas have been preserved to the British Crown." This was indeed a high point in MacNab's career.

The Burning of the Caroline

1. What is happening in this picture?
2. If Commander Drew had been court-martialled for his part in the *Caroline* affair, how would you have defended him?
3. Can you discover which Americans were particularly anxious to assist William Lyon Mackenzie? Why?

Parliament Chapter 13
in Flames

The rebellions of 1837 brought a change of heart in Britain and Lord Durham to Canada. His report recommended the union of the two Canadas and one Assembly with Parliament Buildings in Montreal.

Sir Allan MacNab was elected to this new Legislative Assembly where he was faced with a number of difficult pieces of legislation. Most difficult was the Rebellion Losses Bill. A similar Bill had been passed for Canada West (formerly Upper Canada), but one for Canada East was another matter.

Sir Allan was up to his eyes in this debate. "The Patriots," he cried, "are nothing more than foreigners and rebels. To pay them for their losses during the rebellion is to reward treason!"

"You're a rebel yourself," shouted William Hume Blake, the Member for Toronto, his temper rising.

"And you're a liar," Allan roared back.

At this point, both men climbed out of their seats and rushed across the floor to fight. The gallery, where the spectators sat, roared with shouts and seethed with hisses. The Sergeant-at-Arms pulled them apart only with the greatest difficulty and had them removed.

In due course, the Bill passed its third reading. Lord Elgin, the Governor, acted according to the law of responsible government, newly granted to the United Canadas. He accepted the advice of the elected Legislature and, therefore, gave royal assent to the Bill.

As Elgin left the Houses of Parliament, angry jeers and shouts greeted him, and his carriage was pelted with stones. By the evening, the fire bells of the town called people into the streets. They were given copies of a printed leaflet inviting them to a mass meeting, to be held at eight in the Champ de Mars.

When did newspapers, or news sheets, first appear in the provinces of Canada?

George Moffat was the chairman. "Elgin must be recalled, and the Rebellion Losses Bill cancelled," he said. Other speakers agreed, arguing that their demands should be backed with force.

"On to the Parliament Buildings," shouted someone in the crowd, which now surged out into the streets and was swallowed up in the darkness.

Furniture, lights, and fittings in the hall were smashed in the wild rage of destruction. Gas pipes were broken and burst into flames. Soon the whole building was wrapped in flames, while the so-called respectable citizens of Montreal in top hats and evening coats watched from the sidewalks.

"The building is on fire," shouted a Member in a room in the House, where several others had gone for shelter. Sir Allan MacNab, Sandford Fleming, and three or four more rushed to the wing where the Assembly had been so recently sitting."One of you rescue the mace," ordered Allan. "The rest of you help me carry this painting of Her Majesty." Four of them struggled out with the picture, tears streaming down their faces, and their beards singed by the heat.

"We can't go back into that hell again," decided Sir Allan. "I'm afraid we've lost our precious library and all its 20,000 books and treasures. I could have told you this would happen, if the Governor agreed to that Bill. But he was determined to listen to those Reformers."

"Here come the troops," reported another Member.

"Now perhaps the firemen will be able to bring the fire under control," observed Sandford.

Slowly the troops and armed constables pushed the crowd back, not without cracking a few stubborn heads. Order in the streets was not fully restored until two days later, April 27, 1849. Never again would Parliament be held in Montreal.

A fire engine used at the time of the burning of Parliament.
What were the fire-fighting methods in those days?

The struggling town of Bytown-on-the-Ottawa was chosen as Canada's new capital. Sir Allan had become Speaker of the Legislature in 1846. Now, in 1854, he became Prime Minister of the United Canadas. He had reached the peak of his political career. He held this office for two years. In 1856, his ministers, including John A. Macdonald, resigned. This forced him to do so also.

1. Why was a Rebellion Losses Bill for Canada East "another matter"?
2. What was the major defence against a widespread fire?
3. Where, today, is the portrait of Queen Victoria that MacNab saved?

The Burning of Parliament

Chapter 14 The Great Western Railway

Sir Allan MacNab had more than a political and military career. He was also a highly successful businessman. In 1836, he had founded the Gore Bank (which would eventually become the Canadian Imperial Bank of Commerce); he had interests in the Burlington Bay Dock and Ship Building Company and the Canada Life Assurance Company; and he was a director of the Welland Canal Company.

Allan's greatest love, however, was the railway. In 1834, he helped to pass an Act to form the London and Gore Railway Company. The name was altered by another Act in 1837, and the company was called Great Western.

MacNab knew the value of a railway to a community. He fought for twenty years to have it pass through Hamilton. "Without a railway, industry in Hamilton will never flourish," Allan said. "What fools wish to place it on top of the escarpment? It is natural that it should be at the head of the lake, to funnel not only trade from the United States, but traffic on Lake Ontario."

And so he was to have his way. He had not left the matter to chance, for he personally had raised over $499,000, much of it in Britain, which he often visited. The railway was then lengthened to run from Niagara to Windsor, to provide links with other railways and canals, and to provide a short route through Canada to Detroit.

All this was running through Sir Allan's head, as he stood in the grounds of Dundurn, looking over Burlington Bay on March 19, 1859. Below lay the tracks of his Great Western Railway. The distant sound of a locomotive whistle reached his ears. *She's on time*, he thought, taking his large gold watch out of his vest pocket.

The Toronto, *the first engine built in Ontario, 1853*

How does this total compare with the cost of building the CPR?

What raw products are necessary for the production of iron and steel?

She came round the bend, puffing heavily on the slight upgrade, which led to the bridge over the Desjardins Canal, just out of sight. Great clouds of smoke billowed up, and occasionally a shower of sparks shot upwards when the fireman stoked the boiler. Five passenger carriages trailed the tender, all filled with travellers. Sir Allen waved his hand vigorously as they passed by. It didn't matter that they likely didn't see his greeting or acknowledge it. All that mattered was his pride in the line he had largely helped to create.

What were early passenger train coaches like? How have they developed to today's standards?

These pleasant thoughts were shockingly interrupted by the tortured sound of rending metal and the crash of heavy objects falling to the ground. "Good Lord, there's been an accident!" gasped Allan, with a sickening feeling in the pit of his stomach. Recovering his senses, he rushed off to the castle, to send for his carriage and to see for himself.

In a minute he was on the scene. It was a ghastly one. The engine, *Oxford*, had hit an open switch and jumped the tracks. This had caused part of the bridge to collapse, plunging the locomotive, tender, and two following cars, sixty feet to the ice of the canal below.

"Are there many hurt?" growled Allan, seizing a man roughly by the shoulder.

"They can't say yet, Sir Allan," was the reply.

"They say there are few that aren't hurt, and at least sixty are dead," interrupted another onlooker.

"How many were aboard?" asked Allan.

"They think about three hundred," a third bystander answered.

Sir Allan was not satisfied to stand idly by. He climbed down to the canal level. Bodies were strewn everywhere, and those still alive were being made as comfortable as possible. Horse-drawn ambulances and makeshift wagons were arriving now, as well as doctors called to the scene.

Sir Allan turned over a nearby body, and drew in his breath sharply. "My God!" he blurted out. "It's Sam Zimmerman, my banker friend from Niagara Falls!" The sight of someone he knew so well lying dead made Sir Allan realize the horror of the frightful tragedy.

Sir Allan and his Great Western Railway were to be severely criticized in the newspapers because of the accident. But both the railway and Sir Allan would weather the storm, and move on to greater victories and more prosperous days.

The Great Western Railway from the grounds of Dundurn Castle.

1. Where did the Desjardins Canal go, and why was it built?
2. The canal no longer exists. Can you think why this should have happened?
3. What could have been the causes of this disaster?
4. At what speed did trains travel in the 1850s?

The Desjardins Canal Disaster

Financing the Great Western

1. What are the important facts in this steamship advertisement of 1857? What would be important in a travel advertisement today?
2. What railways exist in Canada today? Plan an advertising campaign for one of them.

A Royal Chapter 15
Visit

Dundurn had experienced many splendid occasions, but none could rival the evening of September 6, 1860. The guest of honour was Albert Edward, Prince of Wales, eldest son of Queen Victoria, and the future King Edward VII.

There had been that memorable night in February, 1841, when sixty sleighloads of men in uniform, and Indians in their ceremonial dress, had come to present him with a broadsword. The sword was a mark of their admiration and respect for his efforts in putting down the Rebellion of 1837.

Then, in November of 1855, the "ambitious city" had recognized his great contribution to their success in bringing the railway to Hamilton. On that occasion, MacNab had been given a wonderful service of twenty-two pieces of plate. An inscription on the centrepiece celebrated his election as Prime Minister; his twenty-five years as Member for the riding; and his work for their material well-being.

Allan MacNab in 1858

There were the family occasions: the brilliant wedding ceremonies of his daughters, Anne Jane and Sophia, in the jewel-like setting of Dundurn, in 1849 and 1855.

But the Prince's visit was the crown of them all. Sir Allan, now a baronet, and aide-de-camp to the Queen, was entertaining the nineteen-year-old Prince, whom Victoria had promised to send to Canada, in gratitude for her loyal support in the Crimean War.

Young Albert Edward, although not at all fond of books and lessons, had great charm and liked people. He threw himself into every activity with all his energy.

"Tomorrow you will be asked to open the new waterworks, Your Royal Highness," said MacNab. "It is a great step forward for the citizens of this city, and one long overdue. It was first planned when Hamilton was struck with the plague, and has only now been finished.

"Then in the afternoon you will open the Crystal Palace," continued Allan.

"Oh, is it like the one my father built in London?" inquired the Prince.

"Very similar,Your Royal Highness, but not as big," replied Sir Allan. "The Crystal Palace is an exhibition hall for art, furniture, fruit and vegetables, baked goods, and even toys. It is located not far from here in the Great Central Fair Grounds and was built by George Mills, a friend of mine."

"And where am I scheduled to appear the following day?" inquired the Prince of Wales, turning to the Duke of Newcastle. The Duke was Secretary of State for the Colonies, and had accompanied the Prince since his arrival in Newfoundland.

"You are to visit Niagara, Your Royal Highness," replied Newcastle.

"And you'll travel on a special coach on my Great Western Railway," chimed in Sir Allan.

"Excellent!" cried the Prince with youthful enthusiasm.

And a joyful day it proved to be. At Queenston, the Prince opened the newly built Brock Monument, which had replaced the one blown up by Irish rebels in 1840. "It looks remarkably like Nelson's Column in Trafalgar Square," remarked Albert Edward.

"It was designed by the same architect," replied Newcastle. Then the Prince unveiled a pillar at the place where Brock fell mortally wounded, and spoke to a number of survivors of the Battle of Queenston Heights. MacNab was in the royal party, and greeted some of his old army friends.

The rest of the day was spent in entertainment, which the Prince shared with some 200,000 other spectators. The greatest tightrope walker who ever lived, a tiny Frenchman called Blondin, was going to cross the gorge of the Niagara River, within sight of the falls.

There was a circus atmosphere on this September 8, 1860. Pedlars had set up their stands everywhere, and were selling every imaginable kind of wares. Con men were busy, as well as pickpockets who hoped to do well in the packed crowds.

Bands were playing, and special stands had been

built, so that people could get a better view. Crowds, ten and twelve deep, also lined the banks of the river for miles.

Once the Prince of Wales was seated in the royal box, draped with patriotic flags, and the band had played "God Save the Queen," Blondin began his act. He walked along the rope, carrying his assistant on his back. Then he crossed again with short stilts attached to his legs. Finally, when halfway across, he swung freely below the rope and then came upright again, quite at his ease.

Many people fainted at the sight. When Blondin reached the platform, the Prince of Wales, looking very pale, presented him with a purse of gold. "Thank God, it is over," he exclaimed, shaking Blondin's hand. "Please never attempt it again!"

Blondin bowed graciously and assured the Prince that there was no danger. "To prove it, Your Royal Highness, allow me to carry you over, or push you across in a wheelbarrow if you prefer," he offered. The Prince smilingly refused, explaining, "I don't think they'd let me, even if I wanted to."

"Good-bye, then, till we meet again, when I perform in London," said Blondin as they parted.

An audience with Queen Victoria at Buckingham Palace.

Blondin crossing Niagara Falls on a tightrope, carrying a man on his back.

The added weight of another man was too much for the tightrope. As Blondin neared the end of the walk, a guy wire snapped. Only Blondin's great skill prevented a tragedy.

What might the conversation be between the two men as Blondin crosses Niagara Falls?

*A wax figure of Blondin
performing a bicycle crossing.*

*Blondin crossing Niagara Falls,
1859.*

Chapter 16 **End of the Line**

Sir Allan MacNab's days had been a series of triumphant processions. He had served his Queen and his nation faithfully and well. He had achieved much and he had left a famous name.

But now his health was breaking down. He had been plagued for years with attacks of gout and racked with pain. He had cursed it, but he had carried on. Now the brave old warrior could fight no longer

One of his last public acts was to attend the funeral of his old friend and companion in arms, William Hamilton Merritt, in St. Catharines in July of 1862. Sir Allan died on Friday, August 8, of "gastric fever."

In death, as in life, he was to be a storm centre, as different churches quarrelled over who should claim him. He had attended Presbyterian and Anglican churches, but his wife was a devout Roman Catholic. Finally, he found a resting place in Holy Sepulchre Cemetery.

Sir Allan Napier MacNab had both praise and blame, but he got things done. And he always remained faithful to his motto, *Gun Eagal* in Gaelic, or *Timor ommis abesto* in Latin, which literally means "Fear Nothing."

44   THE ILLUSTRATED LONDON NEWS   [JAN. 12, 18..]

TESTIMONIAL TO THE HON. SIR ALLAN NAPIER MACNAB.

THIS eminent statesman is the son of a general officer, in the British Army, who, having served his Majesty for many years, went to Canada with his Colonel, the late General Simcoe, the first Governor of Upper Canada. Sir Allan's father greatly distinguished himself, and was repeatedly wounded—having on one occasion had both his legs broken.

During the late war, when the Americans took York (now Toronto), Sir Allan, then a boy between thirteen and fourteen years of age attending the school of Dr. Strachan, now Bishop of Upper Canada, volunteered, with many others, and marched into the woods above the garrison with the Grenadier Company of the King's Regiment, who were nearly all destroyed by the enemy. The army subsequently retreated to Kingston; where, through the influence of the late Gene al Sir R. H. Sheaffe, young Macnab was placed on board Sir James Yeo's ship, on Lake Ontario, as a midshipman, in which capacity he acted under Sir George Prevost at the attack on Sackett's Harbour.

He soon, however, left the Navy, and resumed his position in the Army, joining the 100th Regiment, then in advance on the Niagara frontier. He was at the storming of Fort Niagara and taking of Buffalo and Black Rock, which placed the Niagara frontier in possession of the British; for which services he was honoured with an Ensigncy in the 49th: with this regiment, about the commencement of the Lower Canadian campaign, he marched to Plattsburgh, where he commanded the advanced guard at the bridge over the Saranac on the morning of the attack. He continued to serve with his regiment until the reduction of the Army in 1816, when he returned to Toronto (then York), and commenced the study of the law, with the then Attorney-General.

In 1824, shortly after being called to the Bar, Macnab established himself in Hamilton, then a village of only two hundred inhabitants, where he secured to himself a very lucrative practice, and was the first barrister who was honoured with a silk gown as Queen's Counsel for Upper Canada. In 1828 he had a difficulty with the House of Assembly, by whose order he was committed to custody, but was soon after set at liberty.

In 1830 he was elected to represent the county of Wentworth, in which he resided, in the Provincial Legislature; since which time he has continued in Parliament. He was for several years Speaker of the House of Assembly of the then province of Upper Canada; and is now Prime Minister and leader in the House of Assembly. During the insurrection in Canada in 1837-1838, and when Speaker of the Assembly, Sir Allan command-d the militia force in Upper Canada; and, after the dispersion of the rebels at Gallows-hill, he put down the rebellion in the London district. At one day's notice he marched with 1400 men to the Niagara frontier, where he remained for the greater part of the winter to repel the threatened attack of escaped rebels and American sympathisers and brigands. By his prompt action in cutting out and destroying the piratical steamer Caroline, he put an end to the rebellion and attempted invasion of that part of the province. For these services, so generally known and acknowledged, Sir Allan was knighted.

Sir Allan has always a warm advocate those public improvements which have tended so powerfully to develop the resources and increase the population of Canada.

In 1834 he procured an Act incorporating the London and Gore Railway Company; which was amended by a subsequent Act introduced by him in March 1837, and the name of the Company was changed to that of the Great Western, now known in this country as the Great Western of Canada. Owing to the rebellion which broke out at the commencement of the following winter, and the consequent long period of blight which

fell upon the province, this and all projects for improving its condition remained in abeyance. When better times returned, Sir Allan renewed his exertions on behalf of this and the Grand Trunk line, and was mainly instrumental in procuring for both enterprises the aid of the Provincial Government; which formed the chief element in the success which has attended the construction of these works, now so well known and appreciated. Sir Allan Macnab's mind was also early directed to the importance to the trade of Canada of rendering the St. Lawrence navigable

or lake-going craft of large burden; he also aided materially in carrying on those magnificent canals constructed to avoid the rapids of that mighty river—unsurpassed by any similar works in the world. He likewise supported with all his influence the enlargement of the Welland Canal, which connects the two great lakes, Erie and Ontario, to a capacity to admit of vessels carrying 500 tons, passing from any of the great western lakes through to tide water, and thence to any part of the world.

As early as the year 1835 he turned his attention to the desirability of increasing the facilities of communication between the western lakes and Lake Ontario and the St. Lawrence by means of a railway connection. In that year he procured an Act to incorporate a Company for the purpose, called the Hamilton and Port Dover Railway Company. This line was delayed in its completion from the causes before assigned; but the charter has been recently revived by Sir Allan, and the route is now regarded as likely to become one of the most important channels for the vast and yearly increasing trade of Western America.

In person Sir Allan possesses a commanding and noble aspect, and has ever been remarkable for energy of character, and determination of purpose. In manner and address he is affable; and amidst the turmoil of political strife always commanded the personal esteem and social respect of all parties.

The accompanying Portrait has been engraved, from a photograph by Milne.

The great public service rendered by Sir Allan to his native country, together with his untiring efforts in promoting the interests of Hamilton (now a city of 25,000), lately induced his constituents and friends in other parts of the province to join in presenting him with a handsome Service of Plate as a testimonial of their esteem, and an acknowledgement of his long and faithful services.

The presentation took place at the Hall of the Mechanics' Institute in Hamilton on the 29th October last. The noble apartment, in which was tastefully decorated for the occasion, presented a most brilliant appearance. In all parts of the room the flags of the Allies were blended together in graceful festoons.

On a high stand upon the dais at the end of the room was displayed the costly plate; behind it was placed a large mirror, tastefully decorated with bouquets, and surrounded by union-jacks. Fronting this, and running parallel with the dais, was the chief table, at which George W. Burton, Esq., presided; on his right sat the guest of the evening. Three tables extended the whole length of the room. The demonstration passed off with great éclat, and was attended not only by the leading men of Hamilton, but by others from a distance.

The superb Service of Plate was purchased from Messrs. Lambert and Rawlings, Coventry-street, London. It consists of 22 pieces, with a splendid Candelabrum as a centre piece, bearing the following inscription:—

Presented to Colonel the Honourable Sir ALLAN NAPIER MACNAB, Prime Minister of Canada, who has represented the City of Hamilton and County of Wentworth, in the Parliament of Canada, for twenty-five years, by the Citizens of Hamilton, of all political parties, as an acknowledgment of his valuable services and untiring efforts in promoting the material interests of that City and of the Province generally; but more especially that of the Great Western Railway, which has conferred the most important and lasting benefits—moral, fiscal, and political, upon Hamilton and upon Canada. 1855

The above inscription is also on one side of the large Cup; on the other side of which is " Success to the Great Western Railway of Canada." Around the base of the Candelabrum are the figures of Justice, Peace, and Truth. Peace holds in her right hand a palm leaf, on which is inscribed "G. W. R." (Great Western Railway). Each article bears the Macnab crest, with the motto "Timor omnis abesto."

THE HON. SIR ALLAN MACNAB, PRIME MINISTER OF CANADA.—(FROM A PHOTOGRAPH.)

Testimonial to Sir Allan MacNab

1. *The Illustrated London News* is still published. This page looks very different from today's magazine. What are the chief differences?
2. The picture is a lithograph. How is a lithograph made? What is an etching?
3. The picture was made from a photograph. Early photographs were called daguerreotypes. How did they get this name?

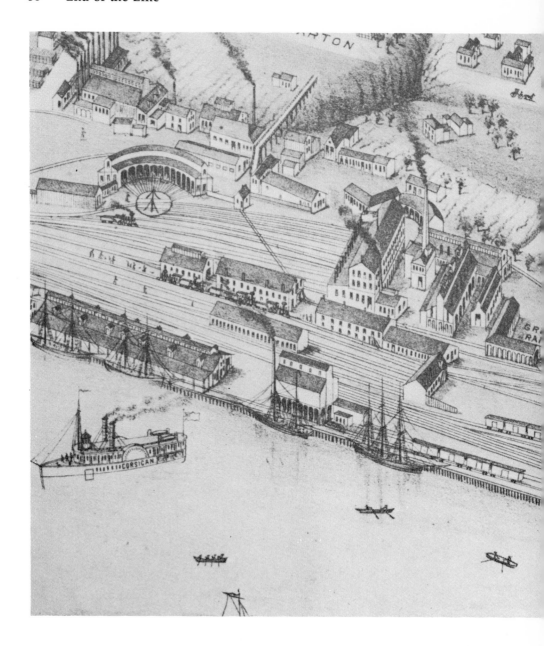

The City MacNab Built

1. Why was Hamilton very suited to be an industrial city?
2. Why was a railway essential to the city's growth?
3. How does the future of a steel-producing city, such as Hamilton, appear to you?

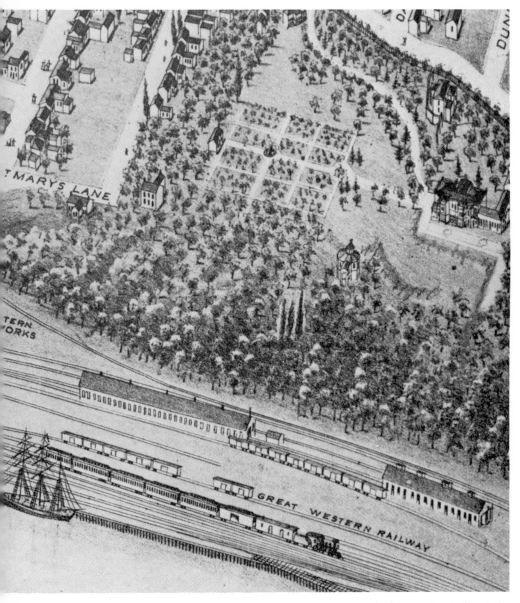

The Great Western Railway train yards in Hamilton.

*Hamilton in the Mid-Nineteenth
Century.*

Credits

The authors would like to express their gratitude to Mrs. Wilson, Reference Librarian at the St. Catharine's Public Library, for her interest and assistance, and Mrs. Caroline Roy who typed the manuscript so ably.

The publishers wish to acknowledge with gratitude the following who have given their permission to use copyrighted illustrations in this book:

The Reverend T. M. Bailey and Mr. C. A. Carter, pages 15, 31 and 49.
The Reverend T. M. Bailey, Mr. C. M. Carter and Mr. Arthur Wallace, Arch., page 17.
Bochsler Studios Ltd., Hamilton, Ontario, page 56.
Dundurn Castle, Hamilton, Ontario, pages 26 and 27.
Hamilton Public Library, pages 25 and 60-61.
The Louis Tussaud Wax Museum, Niagara Falls, pages 52 and 53.
Metropolitan Toronto Central Library, pages 28 and 37.
Public Archives of Canada, pages 1, 2, 3, 6, 8, 9, 10, 14, 29, 30, 33, 34, 38, 42, 44, 47, 53 and 55.
J. Ross Robertson Collection, Metropolitan Toronto Central Library, pages 4 and 13.

Editing: Laura Damania
Design & Illustration: Jack Steiner

Every effort has been made to credit all sources correctly. The authors and publishers will welcome any information that will allow them to correct any errors and omissions.